urgy

by
Bishop Peter J. Elliott

*All booklets are published thanks to the
generous support of the members of the
Catholic Truth Society*

CATHOLIC TRUTH SOCIETY
PUBLISHERS TO THE HOLY SEE

Contents

Understanding the Christian Sacrifice 3

How we offer the sacrifice 4

Where we offer sacrifice 12

The people who offer the sacrifice 20

In Scripture and Tradition 30

The work of Christ, Priest and Lamb 45

Questions to resolve 51

A wondrous mystery 66

Understanding the Christian Sacrifice

From ancient times people have sought to establish union with God by offering sacrifices. What is offered in sacrifice belongs to God and becomes holy. The Latin word *sacrificium*, "sacrifice", is derived from *sacrum facere*, "to make holy". In Catholic liturgy to make something holy is to set it apart by "consecration". We use this word for the central moment of the Mass when the priest says the words of Jesus Christ at the Last Supper over the bread and wine.

To understand the Christian sacrifice given to us at the Last Supper, we first reflect on the shape of the liturgy, actions and symbols, particularly the altar and sacred space set apart for the Eucharistic sacrifice. We focus on the priest and people gathered by God to celebrate this Sacrifice of the Church. We then go to the words of Jesus Christ at the Last Supper, recorded in the Scriptures and passed on across the ages in sacrificial worship which proclaims Christ as Priest and Lamb. Finally we resolve questions such as "Is the Mass a sacrifice or a meal?"

How we offer the sacrifice

The way we celebrate the Liturgy reflects the great truths of the Eucharist: first and foremost the true Sacrifice, of Jesus Christ Priest and Lamb, the change of bread and wine into his Body and Blood and his Real Presence among us. Drawing on the prayers, psalms, rituals and ceremonies of the Jerusalem Temple and the synagogue, Christian liturgical worship developed across three millennia. All these liturgies begin with a proclamation of the word of God.

The *Liturgy of the Word*, the first part of the Roman Rite of the Mass, was once known as the "Liturgy of Catechumens", because those preparing for Baptism were allowed to remain only for this phase of the Eucharistic celebration. It consists of prayers, psalms and readings from the Scriptures, and appears to be based on the worship of the synagogues, adapted by the early Christians and perfected with readings from the New Testament, the Christian Scriptures. The main theme of the Liturgy of the Word is God speaking to us here and now, through the inspired Word of Scripture.

The supreme moments of this part of Mass come at the Gospel, when we all stand to hear the very words of Jesus Christ, present in this communication of his saving message today. On Sundays the Gospel is explained in the homily or sermon; then we express our Faith together in the Creed, the words of the whole Church. After this profession of faith we pray for all people in the Prayer of the Faithful or General Intercessions. But the Liturgy of the Word prepares for and leads into the "holy mysteries" of the Eucharistic Sacrifice.

The fourfold action

The *Liturgy of the Eucharist*, the main part of the Mass, was once known as the "Liturgy of the Faithful", because only those who had been baptised were allowed to remain for the offering of the Lord's Sacrifice when the actions of Christ at the Last Supper are repeated by the priest in four stages.

1. *Jesus Christ took the bread and wine* - the Preparation of the Offerings or Offertory, when the bread and wine are brought to the altar and offered to God for the most sacred purpose.

2. *He consecrated the bread and wine* - the Eucharistic Prayer or Canon of the Mass, when, through the hands of the priest and the words of Christ, bread and wine are changed into his Body and Blood, offered up in Sacrifice for us, taking us into the renewal of his life, death and resurrection.

3. *He broke the bread* - the "fraction" or breaking of the Host, so it may be eaten and shared in Holy Communion, also a sign of his broken Body on the Cross.

4. *He gave this sacred Food to his disciples* - the eating and drinking of his Body and Blood, Holy Communion, when Christ comes to us, we come to him, and are made one in him.

The Liturgy of the Eucharist concludes with prayer in thanksgiving for Holy Communion and the celebrant's blessing. The deacon or celebrant sings or says the dismissal, sending us out into the world to live the life of Christ, to become the One we have received. "*Go in peace, glorifying the Lord with your life*".

The sacrificial action

Another way of understanding the actions and words of Our Lord presents the Sacrifice unfolding in three moments: *Offering, Immolation and Consummation.*

1. *Jesus Christ took the bread and the wine.* This is *the Offering.* In the Preparation of the Offerings or Offertory, the priest presents the bread and wine to God, concluding this action with the Prayer over the Offerings or Secret Prayer in the extraordinary form of Mass.

2. *Jesus Christ gave thanks over the bread and wine.* This is *the Immolation.* The priest prays the Eucharistic Prayer or Canon which centers around the consecration or narrative of institution when the bread and wine are changed into the Body and Blood of the Lord, offered up for us.

3. *Jesus Christ gave his Body and Blood.* This is *the Consummation.* The Communion Rite completes the whole action of Sacrifice as the priest and people enter most fully into it by eating the Body of the Lord and drinking his Blood.

This approach brings together what we do and what Christ the Priest and Lamb does for us and through us in the action of liturgy. But to perceive the Sacrificial heart of this action we reflect on how it has been celebrated across the centuries.

Celebrating towards the East

From the earliest times priests and people celebrated the Eucharist at Christian altars facing East. This custom was symbolic of God's People turning to the Lord, looking towards the rising sun, a sign of the coming of the risen Christ with his light of grace, hope and salvation. To face East usually meant that the priest and people all faced the same way, so the priest was leading the people, not turning his back on them. But if the sanctuary happened to be at the

Western end of the church, then the priest faced the people (e.g. Saint Peter's Basilica, Rome). This was also necessary if the tomb of a saint was set directly in front of the altar (also the plan of Saint Peter's).[1]

The liturgical movement of the past century favored the celebrant facing the people. Some scholars claimed that this was the original way the Eucharist was celebrated. To promote better participation in worship, Mass facing the people was revived before the Second World War in some parishes and monasteries, and especially in student circles in France and Germany where the "dialogue Mass" was introduced.

Celebrating Mass facing the people was endorsed as a favored option in liturgical reforms after the Second Vatican Council. Although the former practice was never abolished, currently it is almost universal for Mass of the Roman Rite to be celebrated with the priest facing the people. This may facilitate communication, but it has given the impression that the celebrant is the host of a meal, rather than a priest offering sacrifice. Scholars now tell us that this was never a widespread practice in the early centuries of Christianity. According to the symbolic mentality of that distant era, the position of priest and people was determined more by their desire to offer sacrifice facing East. They did not think in modern liturgical categories of full and active participation.

Up to the era of Vatican II, most Masses were celebrated with the priest facing the altar. In the light of what has been indicated, it is ignorant to describe this as "the priest with his back to the people". That comment also insults our Eastern Catholic brothers and sisters, because in their liturgies the Eucharistic Sacrifice is offered facing East. We should respect their desire to "turn to the Lord" in humble awe before the mystery of his sacrifice.

Celebrating around the Cross

However, Pope Benedict XVI has shown a way to "turn to the Lord" whenever Mass is celebrated facing the people. This involves a simple rearrangement of the altar, what some call the "Benedictine Altar". At all papal Masses, the crucifix now stands at the centre, no longer to one side. It is flanked by candles of a significant size. As a theologian Pope Benedict had argued that the altar is not a setting to display a man (Pope, bishop or priest), rather, during the sacrificial action of the liturgy, the altar itself should draw us around Jesus Christ crucified and risen.[2] Once you place the crucifix at the centre of the altar, it becomes visually "an altar", not just a fine table adorned with candles and flowers.

The altar crucifix is a vivid symbol of the Eucharistic Sacrifice. It is placed on, behind, above or near the altar, always visually related to the altar. In the revised *General Instruction of the Roman Missal* it is defined as a cross "with a figure of Christ crucified".[3] This excludes not only an empty cross but also using a figure of the risen Christ as the altar cross. Not only is this crucifix to be clearly visible, but it is fitting that it remain on or near the altar outside the time of liturgical celebrations. A processional crucifix may serve as the altar cross.

The great prayer

We celebrate liturgy not only through signs and symbols, but through words, in prayers. Some prayers are fixed, others change with the day or season; some are said, others sung; some we can hear, others are said quietly. The whole liturgy can be understood as one continuous prayer made up of many components. Hence, the Sacrifice of Jesus Christ in the Mass is *the* perfect prayer. In this the Great Prayer of the whole Church all our personal prayers are caught up by Jesus the High Priest offering himself in self-giving love to the Father in the Spirit.

However, here we have to be honest. None of us finds praying easy all the time or even most of the time. But at every celebration of the Eucharistic Sacrifice we "tune into" a Prayer that is infinitely greater than our own prayers, *the* greatest prayer, a prayer that makes up for, absorbs and refines our distracted thoughts and words. In a sense, we "lean on" or depend on the endless prayer of the Eucharistic Sacrifice, an unceasing prayer of praise and thanksgiving, of intercession and atonement, that continues at every second of the day, "*from the rising of the sun to its setting*", as the "*pure sacrifice*" is made (cf. Eucharistic Prayer III).

This approach can be useful when young people say that they are bored at Mass or find they cannot "get anything out of it". They are discouraged by the standard adult reply "You don't put enough into it" because the Great Prayer does not depend on our efforts or emotions. The Great Prayer draws us into the mystery. It is a moment of grace, not depending on human effort or how we happen to feel at the time.

While we should all "pray the Mass", at the same time we need to let the supernatural power, wonder and mystery of the Mass carry us along. The full active participation called for at Vatican II really means a deeper spiritual experience, worship "*in spirit and in truth*". The Mass points us towards eternal life where worship and being will be one.

Where we offer sacrifice

The place where the Eucharist is celebrated proclaims that Christian liturgy is the Lord's Sacrifice. At the heart of every Catholic church is an altar. In remote regions of the world the church may be a simple structure containing only one fixed object - the altar. Every church is constructed primarily to hold an altar. A church may be defined as covered space where the community is gathered by God to do what Jesus Christ commanded at the Last Supper, to offer his sacrifice.

Nevertheless, the Lord's Sacrifice can be celebrated anywhere. No specific place is required for Christ's universal act of worship *"in spirit and in truth"*. In emergency situations, for example during persecution, Mass has been offered in factories, restaurants, in prisons and concentration camps, in caves or in fields on the "Mass rocks" of Ireland. There are pastoral provisions for Mass to be celebrated outside a church, for example in a house, a longstanding custom in Ireland. But under normal circumstances the liturgy is celebrated in a dedicated church, the sacred space where God gathers his people for worship at a dedicated altar.

Most of the furnishings of a church are derived from the altar and relate to the altar: the ambo or lectern for the proclamation of the word, the chair for the presiding priest, the tabernacle for reserving the Blessed Eucharist, places for the people, servers and choir.

The symbolism of the Christian Altar

Most religions have an "altar", usually a table, pedestal or stand, where priests offer sacrifices to God or gods. The Old Testament includes many references to stone structures where sacrifices of animals, wheat, fruit etc. were offered and then usually burnt. Contact between the victim and the altar was part of the ritual. The altar was regarded as a kind of portal to heaven.

However, at the Last Supper Jesus Christ ended the sacrifices offered at such an altar. He changed the Passover into his sacrifice for a new Israel, the Church. When he gave himself up as the "Lamb of God" at the Last Supper, a domestic table became an altar. When he accomplished his atoning and reconciling work for us the next day, a criminal's cross became an altar. That cross pointed to another "altar" beyond this world. In the Letter to the Hebrews he himself is the temple and altar. All this redefinition of the altar flowed into the Eucharistic Sacrifice. In every church the altar is a silent witness to the Lord's Sacrifice.[4]

Therefore, the Christian altar has been described as the "great sign of Christ". This is why it is placed in a central position and why it is meant to be an object of beauty and splendor, worthy of the Lord's Sacrifice. It is also a permanent object, one reason why most Catholic altars are fixed to the floor and constructed of stone or marble. Christ is the Rock of his People, God and Man with us for ever, always among us.

The symbolism of the altar as "the great sign of Christ" is revealed when it is dedicated by the bishop. The new altar is first sprinkled with holy water, then anointed with the most sacred oil, Holy Chrism, crowned with a blazing fire of fragrant incense and dedicated, set apart, with a solemn prayer. These are all signs of the work and presence of the Holy Spirit, who is one with Our Lord, "the Christ", the "anointed One". Henceforth, this anointed table of marble, stone or wood can only be used for one purpose – the offering of the Eucharistic Sacrifice.

After it has been dedicated the altar is dressed with the cloths and candles that are used at every celebration of the Eucharist. Finally, something greater than symbolism takes place: the real dedication of the altar. Mass is celebrated on it for the first time. Here we pass beyond symbolism, for Christ himself becomes really, truly and substantially present among us in the celebration of his Sacrifice.

The Christian altar is not only the holy table of sacrifice. As the beautiful prayers of dedicating an altar remind us, it is at the same time the holy table of the Supper of the Lamb, where the faithful come to receive the Body and Blood of Christ, to be nourished in the Eucharistic banquet.

The Lord's Table on earth is a foretaste of the heavenly banquet – "*blessed are those called to the supper of the Lamb*".

The altar itself thus draws together the two complementary dimensions of the Mass – sacrifice and banquet. At this sacred table, Jesus Christ offers up his Body and Blood for the living and the dead. From this sacred table he gives us his Body and Blood to be our food of eternal life.

History of the Christian Altar

Saint Paul speaks of the "*table of the Lord*" in 1 Corinthians 10:21, although this refers more to the Eucharist than to the place where it is celebrated. But the words "we have an *altar*" in Hebrews 13:10 could be the earliest reference to the Eucharistic table as an "altar" because this altar is a place where food is eaten. In post-apostolic times, early in the Second Century, Ignatius of Antioch used the Greek word for "altar", *thusiasterion* to refer to the celebration of the Eucharist by the bishop and also to the place where the holy sacrifice is offered. This word is derived from the Greek Septuagint text of the Old Testament, where it describes the places where the Hebrew people offered their sacrifices.

The first Christians used two Greek words to describe their Eucharistic tables: *thusiasterion*, meaning "altar", and *trapeza* meaning table. The words thus express the twofold meaning of the Mass, sacrifice and banquet. The Latin Fathers used the standard words for an altar, *ara* and *altare*, not only to refer to the Eucharist itself but to the holy table where the mysteries are celebrated. While Tertullian used *ara*, Saint Cyprian took this word to refer to a pagan altar, and preferred *altare*, the Latin origin of our English word "altar".

The earliest Christian altars were made of wood, probably because Mass was first celebrated in people's homes. In the grander Roman villas a stone table was used as the altar, and the plan of the church may still reflect the plan of a villa.[5] By the Fourth Century, when Christianity was legal and many churches were being built, altars were constructed of stone, marble or alabaster. A stone altar is a sign of a permanent place of sacrifice linking us with our Jewish heritage, because altars described in the Old Testament were made of stones.

The Christian altar was always treated with great reverence. The Greek Fathers described the "holy table" as "mystical", "tremendous" and "priestly". It was regarded as so holy that nothing was allowed to be placed on it except the sacred vessels for the Eucharist, the chalice and paten, and the holy book of the gospels.

As we see in a mosaic of Melchisedech in Ravenna, an altar of the fifth or sixth century was usually cube-shaped, freestanding, dressed in rich hangings and embroidered cloths. Candles stood around it and above it were suspended a jeweled cross and lamps. It came to be enshrined under a canopy, resting on four columns, the *ciborium* or the *baldachino* that we still see in great Roman basilicas such as Saint Peter's. Silken veils hanging from this canopy were drawn around the altar during the sacred moments of the consecration out of reverence for the offering of the Sacrifice.

This canopy and its veils echo the Holy of Holies in the Temple which in turn is reflected in the canopy set above a bride and groom at a Jewish wedding.[6] Christ the Bridegroom gives himself up in love for his bride the Church and this Great Mystery of self-sacrifice is contained in the Eucharist. "The Church is his beloved Bride who calls to her Lord, and through him offers worship to the eternal Father."[7]

The sanctuary

The altar was always located in an area set apart from the rest of the church, the "sanctuary" or holy place. This expresses a universal religious instinct, that sacred space should be reserved for the offering of sacrifice, evident both in the Temple of Jerusalem and in pagan temples. But a Christian church was more like a synagogue than a temple, that is, a roofed building to house people for community worship and instruction. Yet the sense of a temple is retained in a raised area reserved for the altar.

To define that area, the sanctuary was separated from the rest of the church by a low screen, as may still be seen in old Roman basilicas such as San Clemente or Santa Maria in Cosmedin. In the Byzantine East this screen was adorned with icons and gradually developed into the *ikonostasis*, the high solid screen that conceals the sanctuary and altar during the sacred rites of the Greeks, Ukrainians, Russians etc., Catholics and Orthodox. By concealing a sacred place for sacrificial action, the mystery or supernatural event is emphasized. The altar and sanctuary in the Christian East thus symbolize the heavenly altar in the Letter to the Hebrews, just as the way the liturgy is celebrated reflects the angelic worship of heaven. Christians are raised into the heavenly dimension each time they come before the sanctuary for the Divine Liturgy.

In the West, where the Roman Rite prevailed, the altar was brought closer to the back wall, losing its cubical form and becoming longer. Behind it rose a reredos adorned with paintings, carvings or sculpture. An open screen separated the sanctuary and choir (clergy and singers) from the nave where the people assembled. In England this screen was crowned with a large crucifix, the rood. To pass under this symbol of Christ crucified was to enter the place where his sacrifice was celebrated. In the seventeenth and eighteenth centuries fewer screens were built because of a desire to see the Mass, but the sanctuary was marked off by altar rails. After post-Vatican II liturgical changes, the sanctuary is still defined in some way.[8] The altar of sacrifice always has its own sacred space.

In the Middle Ages, a cross, candles and relics began to be placed on the altar. But, with some exceptions, the tabernacle for reserving the Eucharist was not set on an altar until the Sixteenth Century. Before that time the tabernacle took various forms: a Eucharistic tower, a small shrine suspended over the altar (the hanging pyx, often shaped like a dove) or a noble safe set in a wall (the aumbry). Placing flowers on the altar or on shelves behind it seems to date from the Eighteenth Century. All these developments show reverence for the Eucharistic Sacrifice.

Reverence for the altar was part of the Eucharistic faith of the Christians over the centuries. They took great care to build noble altars. Unfortunately, today some of our churches contain altars that are not significant or beautiful. Therefore, liturgists encourage us to build truly worthy and noble altars for the celebration of the Eucharistic Sacrifice.

The people who offer the sacrifice

So far we have focused on the shape of the liturgy, sacrificial symbols and the sacred space set aside for the Lord's Sacrifice. But the personal dimensions of the Eucharist were central when Jesus Christ freely gave himself up for us, and commanded his apostles to "*do this in memory of me*". What we do in liturgy helps us see what the Lord does for us.

The sacrificing priests

A priest offers a sacrifice. By his command to "*do this in memory of me*" Jesus Christ ordained the men at the supper table as priests of his New Covenant. This teaching of the Council of Trent becomes clear once we understand his words as a divine command, a creative word of God like "Let there be light!" or "Go, baptize!" When God commands, something happens. God empowers. Jesus Christ was saying "Now you are my priests and you can do this!"

Their new priesthood may be described as a "Melchisedech priesthood", a priesthood based on the Lord's powerful word. This permanent priesthood derived from a divine act is symbolized by a mysterious royal figure who presented bread and wine before Abraham (cf.

Genesis 14: 18-20). *"The Lord has sworn and will not repent, you are a priest for ever according to the order of Melchisedech"* (Psalm 110:4). This "Tu es sacerdos" is chanted as a prayer for priests.

The apostles shared in Christ's priesthood. He is the true Priest. They can only act in and for him. Today, at the altar their successors the bishops and priests act "in the person of Christ". In a sense it might even be said that they "impersonate" the Lord. But their sacred role is no charade. Acting in and for Christ, these men "put on Christ", symbolized when they assume sacred vestments that minimize the celebrant's personality. His role at the altar must also make sense as a visible image and sign of the historical Christ, another reason why the Catholic priest is male. Moreover their ordination builds on a permanent sharing in the Priesthood of Christ that is received by every Christian in Baptism.

At the hands of these apostolic priests, bread and wine is changed into his Body and Blood. As they obey him and *"do this"*, they bring before the Father that perfect Sacrifice that the Lord Jesus offered on the cross for all humanity. In the Fourth Eucharistic Prayer, the celebrant addresses God the Father, *"we offer you his Body and Blood, the sacrifice acceptable to you which brings salvation to the whole world."*

Through his sacrificing priests Christ the Priest provides one universal sacrifice to replace sacrifices that could only be offered in the Temple, or once a year at Passover. The universal Eucharistic Sacrifice can be celebrated at any time and in any place, This pure and universal offering or oblation was prophesied before Christ walked the earth (cf. Malachi 1:11). This is echoed in the Third Eucharistic Prayer: "...*you never cease to gather a people to yourself, so that from the rising of the sun to its setting a pure sacrifice may be offered to your name.*" This is when "*true worshippers will worship the Father in spirit and truth*" as Our Lord revealed to the Samaritan woman when she tried to argue about the "correct" places for offering sacrifice (cf John 4: 19-26).

A ministerial priesthood

The one leading or presiding over every celebration of the Eucharist is called a "priest", meaning one who offers sacrifice. Logically that suggests that the Eucharistic celebration is a sacrifice. But the celebrant of the Mass is not a priest of the old Temple. The priesthood received by the apostles was different.

The apostles could not be Temple priests because this priesthood of Aaron was inherited, based on membership in the tribe of Levi. The duties of priests in the tabernacle in the wilderness and later in the Temple of Jerusalem revolved around the ritual functions of offering various sacrifices of animals, birds or food, with external ritual acts, such as killing, sprinkling blood, burning the offerings as a holocaust. But that system had been brought to an end at the Last Supper.

Guided by what Christ taught and did, his first priests had to abandon this merely cultic idea of priesthood. At the Last Supper Jesus revealed his new priesthood not as some function a man can take up or set aside but as a permanent consecration. Through loving service and self-giving, these consecrated men modeled their lives on the self-giving love of the Redeemer Priest, who is for ever a compassionate High Priest.

When he knelt to wash the feet of fishermen the true Priest showed them his *ministerial* priesthood, that is, priesthood as service of others. So while his command to "do this" was a creative divine command, ordaining them to his new priesthood for ever, it was also a call to serve. Indeed it was a call to ultimate service, to lay down one's life like the Good Shepherd who "does this" for his flock. At same time they are the male icons of Jesus the Bridegroom who "*gave himself up*" for his beloved bride, the Church by laying down his life in sacrifice.

The Eucharist is always the great source of sacrificial service, the source of grace, spiritual energy to keep serving others. Men being ordained to offer this One Sacrifice receive the paten with bread and the chalice of wine from the bishop, who says, "*Accept from the holy people of God the gifts to be offered to him. Know what you are doing and imitate the mystery you celebrate: model your life on the mystery of the Lord's cross."*

Called to model their lives on the mystery that passes through their anointed hands, the self-giving love of the victim and servant who came "not to be served but to serve", priests make an acceptable sacrifice of their lives. Day by day they are called to place themselves, as it were, on the paten and in the chalice, as they pray with and for the people they serve. They are called to proclaim and explain the saving word of God to these people, to bring pardon and peace to them in the Sacrament of Penance and Reconciliation, to anoint them with the oil of healing and forgiveness. Yet the source of their ministry of reconciliation is always the Eucharist, the saving sacrifice of Christ's Cross, his perfect act of reconciliation between God and humanity.

Therefore the priests of Jesus Christ take upon themselves the selfless service and care of the Good Shepherd who knows and loves all his sheep, even laying down his life for them. As they act in the Person of Christ, as an *alter Christus* (another Christ), priests are called to identify, as Jesus did, with their people in times of anguish and pain, loneliness, sorrow and joy.

The priestly people

When the priest offers Mass he is not isolated from the people. He acts as a member of the Church, a man called from the priestly people of God to serve this people. He is raised into a special share in Christ's eternal Priesthood by the sacrament of Holy Orders for the sake of the people. The Second Vatican Council teaches: *"Through the ministry of priests the spiritual sacrifice of the faithful is completed in union with the sacrifice of Christ the only mediator, which in the Eucharist is offered through the priest's hands in the name of the whole Church in an unbloody and sacramental manner until the Lord himself comes."* [9]

How then do the lay faithful offer the Eucharistic Sacrifice? The people offer the Lord's Sacrifice through and with the priest, uniting themselves to him. At the altar he is both the representative of Jesus Christ, acting "in the Person of Christ", and their representative, acting on behalf of God's People as they assemble in prayer before the Father. This is why he uses the first person plural "we" in the public prayers of the liturgy.

The faithful share a communal priesthood through Baptism, and in faith they offer themselves with Christ to the Father in union with the Holy Spirit. Gathered with the priest, they exercise the sharing in the one Priesthood of Christ that they received in Baptism. The Mass is their Sacrifice, but only with and through the sacrificing priest. This why the celebrant says: *"Pray brothers and sisters that my sacrifice and yours may be acceptable to God the almighty Father."* Standing, as if to say, "We are present!" the people respond, *"May the Lord accept the sacrifice at your hands to the praise and glory of his name, for our good and the good of all his holy Church.*"

Apart from a priest, the people cannot offer the Eucharistic sacrifice. Apart from them his sacrifice would not be that of the Church. Yet this does not mean a Mass is invalid if no people are present. Even when a priest celebrates the Eucharist alone, he is offering the worship of the whole Church, a visible community on earth, a wider unseen community of Blessed Mary and all the saints in eternity.

However the people who offer the Eucharistic sacrifice do not come together just by their own efforts, "gathering" for the Eucharist as if this were something we do for ourselves. Pope Benedict XVI has reminded us that it is God who gathers us, just as God gathered his chosen people by calling them out of Egypt into the wilderness...[10] Moses told Pharaoh to "*let my people go*" but for a specific purpose, to offer sacrifice to the true God out in the desert (cf. Exodus 7:16). There God taught them to worship in a prescribed way and gave them the covenant Law, his Ten Words or commandments to guide them to live as his chosen People.

At the Last Supper Christ prescribed the worship of those he called and gathered together to be his new People, a new covenant sacrifice with a new Law. To fulfil this sublime action, the Father assembles us at every Mass. As the Third Eucharistic Prayer puts it: "*you never cease to gather a people to yourself"* later describing the gathered people as *"this family whom you have summoned before you"*.

The sacrifice of the Church

The celebration of the Liturgy has been described as the offering of the whole Mystical Body of Christ. As Pope Pius XII and the Second Vatican Council taught, the Mass is the Sacrifice of the Church. While the baptized people and ordained priests exercise the priesthood of Christ in different ways, they act as one body, offering one sacrifice. All of us are taught to offer ourselves with Christ in the Mass, hence to go from the altar and offer our lives for others, where we live and work, day by day. What applies to ordained men, in different ways applies to all gathered by God to celebrate the Eucharist. All are called to loving service, to self-giving love, self-sacrifice.

Gathered by God, Christians take their place in the Eucharistic community at the altars of our churches. They are baptized, confirmed, and ordained, precisely to *"do this in memory of me"*. Three sacraments that carry a permanent effect in us shape the Church for Eucharistic worship. The sacraments of Christian Initiation, Baptism and Confirmation, with Holy Orders lead up to and into the Eucharistic celebration. Thus the Second Vatican Council described the Liturgy as the *"summit and source"* of the life of the whole Church, whether celebrated in each "particular church" or diocese and every parish all around the world. There are dramatic moments when people and pastors experience a greater sense of this "whole Church at worship", for example during Masses celebrated by Pope Benedict when he visited England and Scotland in 2010, and during the liturgies celebrated at World Youth Day.

The liturgies of the Church proclaim that the Divine Liturgy is the Sacrifice of the Church. Particularly in Eastern liturgies, as a "priestly people set apart" the Church offers and enters the heavenly worship of the Trinity here on earth.

The sacrifice of unity and reconciliation

The word "liturgy" is derived from the Greek *leitourgia*, meaning a public duty. The worship of God is a public duty, a public service, an action, in this case the public worship of the whole Church.

In the Eucharistic Sacrifice, the Church fulfils her great public duty, to pray for the world. Offered in a fractured, confused and distracted world, the Mass is the reconciling Sacrifice of the Church, In the Third Eucharistic Prayer God the Father is addressed with these words: "*Look, we pray, on the oblation of your Church and, recognizing the sacrificial Victim by whose death you willed to reconcile us to yourself, grant that all who are nourished by the Body and Blood of your Son and filled with his Holy Spirit, may become one body, one spirit in Christ.*" Then this 'theme' expands in a cosmic way: "*May this sacrifice of our reconciliation, we pray O Lord, advance the peace and salvation of the entire world.*" Yet this is the world God loves, so we pray in hope, offering the perfect prayer God has entrusted to his Church.

However this reconciling sacrifice is always completed by the holy banquet which establishes communion with God and communion with one another. Echoing St Paul, the Fourth Eucharistic Prayer asks that "*all who partake of this one Bread and one Chalice… gathered into one body by the Holy Spirit… may truly become a living sacrifice in Christ to the praise of your glory.*"

The Church is a community made one through the Eucharist. As sacrifice and sacrament, the Eucharist is the cause of her unity. In light of this, Holy Communion is never just a private matter of "I receive the Lord Jesus". Communion is personal, but at the same time it is communal. Our offering together and eating together establishes communion with God and communion with the whole Church. This is why the liturgy reminds us that we celebrate "together with" our Pope, Bishops and priests, with all our brothers and sisters in the communion of the Universal Church. This Church is a communion of particular churches, each in communion with the particular church of Rome. This is why "receiving Communion" is reserved for those who are already "in communion" with one another in the Universal Church.[11]

In Scripture and Tradition

When he instituted the Eucharist, Jesus Christ gave his Church a new sacrifice to offer and he entrusted it to his apostles. Reclining with him at the supper table "on the night before he died", these men may not have understood that this was happening at that moment, because he was yet to be crucified and had not yet risen from the dead. But watching and listening amidst the flickering lamps, they would have understood basically what Jesus was saying and doing, drawing on the language, customs and traditions of their own Hebrew culture.

Last Supper, New Sacrifice

They heard Jesus say: *"This is my body given up for you… This is my blood shed for you."* These words immediately spoke to them of a sacrificed victim, resonating with daily sacrifices offered at that time in the Temple of Jerusalem. The words would take on a precise meaning because they were sharing in the annual ritual of the Passover meal.[12] But the Lord Jesus was changing the sacrifices of Temple and Passover. He was bringing them to completion by instituting one new universal sacrifice that could be offered anywhere at any time. Listening to him and watching his actions, the disciples knew that what Jesus did with the unleavened bread of Passover and a chalice of wine involved some new kind of sacrifice.

The disciples are first commanded to "*take and eat*" the unleavened bread, which is now "*my body*", and to drink this wine, which is now "*my blood*". As he said those words, the disciples heard their Master describing himself in the state of a sacrificed victim. His life force, his blood, is separated from his flesh, drained from his body, like an animal sacrificed in a temple. His blood is shed or "*poured out*" and his body is "*given up for you and for many*".

We hear these words said by a priest at the consecration in every Mass but first we should note that the Body and Blood of Christ is not given "*to* you". That will be the final stage of the liturgical action, the sacred meal, Holy Communion. First his body and blood are offered up "*for* you", handed over, in sacrifice. As we reflect in detail on Christ's Eucharistic words, we can enter more deeply into the mysteries of this Sacrifice which Catholics celebrated in the liturgy.

The scriptural sources

The Eucharistic Words of Christ were taken from the Scriptures and edited by the Church for her liturgies, in the West, mainly the Roman Rite, and in the East, in the Byzantine, Chaldean, Armenian, Syrian, Egyptian and related Rites. We will concentrate on the "words of institution or consecration" in the Roman Rite.

In the ordinary form of the Roman Rite the priest takes the bread into his hands and says, *"Take this, all of you, and eat of it, for this is my Body which will be given up for you."* Then he takes the chalice of wine and says: *"Take this all of you, and drink from it, for this is the chalice of my Blood, the blood of the new and eternal covenant, which will be poured out for you and for many for the forgiveness of sins. Do this in memory of me."*

The scriptural sources for these words are a Letter of Saint Paul and three of the Gospels. In the New Testament, 1 Corinthians 11: 23-25 is the first recorded version of the Eucharistic words of Our Lord. This is the Last Supper tradition that St Paul "received" in those first church communities of Jerusalem and Antioch and then "handed on" to the Corinthian Christians. The next recorded texts would be in the Synoptic Gospels, Mark 14: 22-24, Matthew 26: 26-28 and Luke 22: 19-20. Luke is closer to Paul's 1 Corinthians text, no doubt due to Luke's personal association with Saint Paul and with the churches he founded around the Mediterranean.

"This is my Body… "

Jesus the Christ says, *"This is my Body"*, *"This is the chalice of my Blood"* The Church has taken him literally. He did not say "this symbolizes my body" or "this means my body". He spelt out his Real Presence in his great

Eucharistic discourse in John 6: 25-29, "*my flesh for the life of the world...*"

The brief form "*this is my Body*" in Mark 14:22 is used at the consecration of the bread in the extraordinary form of the Roman rite of the Mass. This is to be expected, given the tradition that Mark's Gospel was written in Rome by a disciple of Saint Peter. In Matthew's Gospel the same brief form appears, also to be expected given the links between the Gospels of Mark and Matthew.

The real change of bread and wine and Christ's Real Presence in the Eucharist are explained in other booklets in this series. Our emphasis here is on the sacrifice that is celebrated and offered at the altar, yet we will see that the change of bread and wine into his Body and Blood is at the heart of the sacrificial action in the liturgy.

"for this is my Body which will be given up for you..."

In the post-Vatican II rite of Mass, "*which will be given up for you*" was added to "*this is my body*". By this decision, Pope Paul VI emphasized the sacrificial meaning of the Eucharist. To be "*given up*", means to be offered up, or to be handed over, consigned or delivered.[13] Christ was handed over to be crucified, delivered into the hands of the Romans. The sacrificial meaning of being handed over, or given into the hands of others, emerges in the words "*for you*". But we turn to St Paul to discern the deeper sacrificial meaning of Jesus being given up for our sake.

Literally translated, 1 Corinthians 11:23 would be, "*this is the body which is - on behalf of you*". The omitted word is presumably "given". In literal English, Luke 22: 19 would be "*this is my body which is being given for you*". Luke used the simple Greek verb for giving. The Latin future *tradetur* "will be given up" comes from the Vulgate Bible. This is the source of the words "*which will be given up for you*" in the Eucharistic Prayers.

In his Letter to the Galatians Saint Paul first used the simple Greek verb for "giving" to express Christ's sin-bearing self-sacrifice: "*Christ having given himself for our sins.*" (Galatians 1:4). But he went on to use stronger language expressing sacrificial offering or immolation: "*The Son of God who loved me and gave himself up for me.*" (Galatians 2:20). A different Greek verb is used here, literally meaning "*giving himself up for me*".[14] This is what is intended at the consecration of the bread in the liturgy.

In a beautiful way "*given up*" links the Holy Eucharist to the Sacrament of Marriage. In the Letter to the Ephesians the same Greek word is used for the Jesus Christ the Bridegroom who is giving himself in love for his beloved spouse the Church: "*Christ loved the Church and gave himself for her*". (Ephesians 5:25). At the beginning of the same chapter, Paul challenges the Ephesians to "*walk in love, as Christ loved us and gave himself up for us, a fragrant offering and sacrifice to God.*" (Ephesians 5: 2).

What is love but total self giving? And there is no greater love than self-sacrifice, to lay down one's life for friends. (cf. John 15:13). In the light of his Resurrection, the friends of the Lord understood that the self-sacrifice of their beloved Master was God's perfect atonement for the sins of the whole world. They expressed this in letters and gospels that come down to us today as the New Testament. But above all they celebrated and shared Christ's selfless love when they obeyed his command to "*do this in memory of me.*"

Sacrifice seems obvious in "*my Body which will be given up for you*". However, in the Sixteenth Century an ambiguous version of these words appeared in Thomas Cranmer's *Book of Common Prayer*: "*this is my body which is given for you*". That could simply refer to the gift of the Eucharist to us, that is, the Body of the Lord given for us to eat, sacred food *for our benefit*. That would suit Cranmer's intentions because he sought to eliminate the Catholic belief in the Sacrifice of the Mass. However sharing the Body and Blood of Christ is not what is first conveyed by "*given up for you*". These words resound with the sacrificial significance of the cross, an offering made *for* us for the remission of our sins, now perpetuated in sacramental form in the Mass. Furthermore, "*my body given up for you*" is in harmony with the vivid sacrificial language that we find when we reflect on the consecration of the wine.

> *"Take this, all of you, and drink from it, for this is the chalice of my Blood, the Blood of the new and eternal covenant, which will be poured out for you and for many, for the forgiveness of sins."*

The Blood of the New Covenant is *"poured out for you and for many for the forgiveness of sins"*. As we noted hearing these words, the disciples would immediately recognize the language of the Temple, where animal sacrifices were offered to God for various purposes. But they heard their beloved Master making himself the sacrificial victim, offering his own blood, his life force, for them, *"for you"* his brethren reclining at table, and for *"many others"*.

At the same time, he is offering himself freely and intentionally. He takes on the active role of the high priest, not only the passive role of a sacrificial victim. His words define the purpose or "end" of his self-sacrifice. *"My blood"* is *"the blood of the new and eternal covenant, which will be poured out for you and for many, for the forgiveness of sins"*.

"The Blood of the new and eternal covenant"

Here we return to the Old Testament, to the first Covenant between God and his chosen People. In the ancient Middle East, a covenant was bestowed by a greater party on a lesser party, a gift, but binding both parties with conditions and obligations. Having led his people out of Egypt into the wilderness, Moses received the Law in the Ten Words or Ten Commandments, the content of the Covenant, a new way of life guided by God. Moses then bound the people to God's covenant by offering animal sacrifices. To seal the covenant, he sprinkled the blood proclaiming, "*This is the blood of the covenant that the Lord has made with you, containing all these rules*". (Exodus 24: 3-8). This is echoed in the words of Jesus, "*the blood of the new and eternal covenant*".[15]

Jesus the Christ takes on the role of a new Moses by establishing a new alliance or agreement between God and a new people, sealed in his own Blood. Thus we can understand how participating in this new covenant sacrifice draws people into a new relationship with God.

At the Last Supper, Jesus immediately defined the purpose of his sacrifice, the remission or forgiveness of sins. This may also be described as a sacrifice in expiation of sins, a propitiation for sins, a sin-bearing sacrifice or an act of atonement. His Body and Blood are offered up "*for the remission of sins*", but at the same time this gift of gracious forgiveness binds the faithful to this new covenant relationship with God. Their new way of life is formed by Christ's New Law of Love and his Beatitudes that reinterpret and fulfil the Ten Commandments of the Old Law. But does this covenant apply to all people?

"My Blood... poured out for you and for many, for the forgiveness of sins."

In the Eucharistic words of Jesus we hear that his sacrifice is offered "for many". Pope Benedict XVI directed that these words be translated literally from the Latin original in all future translations of the Missal, replacing "for all" in English. Why?

Christ died for all, but in the Eucharistic Sacrifice the benefit or "fruit" of his sacrifice is received by "many others", that is, by those who are moved by God's grace to claim all that the Cross contains, those who accept Christ's work of redemption. Therefore, when "for many" is properly understood, there is no suggestion of a denial of the good news that Christ died for all.

However, as devout Jews, the twelve men at the supper table would have had a serious problem with the idea of *drinking* the poured-out Blood of Jesus. In Jewish tradition "the blood is the life" (Deuteronomy 12:23, Leviticus 17:11). As the life-force, blood is offered to God in sacrifices and used for purification from sins. This life force belongs to God alone, the Source of all life; therefore blood could never be consumed by human beings. This is still the kosher food law, which is why Jews only eat meat from which the blood has been drained.

Jesus the Christ went beyond the rules of the Old Covenant and led his disciples into a New Covenant. The disciples would learn that eating his Body, under the appearance of bread, and drinking his Blood, under the appearance of wine, was the great sacrament of his New Law, uniting them to Christ's life force. Through the sacrament they become dependent on him, like branches on a vine (cf. John 15: 1, 4-5) and they gain supernatural life. This grace is stronger than death, the bread of eternal life and his blood: *"he who eats my flesh and drinks my blood has eternal life, and I will raise him up on the last day."* (John 6:54).

"Do this in memory of me"

Finally, from Christ's lips came the Eucharistic command *"Do this in memory of me"*. We just hear a direction. The Jewish ears of the disciples would hear something more - empowering words and a mandate to carry out a new kind of Passover. His last meal with them was a Passover. That was no accident. He timed the supper and his death to coincide with the domestic liturgy that recalled the liberation of the Jews, when they were led by Moses from slavery in Egypt. But now Jesus gives his disciples the mandate to carry out a new memorial for a much greater liberation.

"Do this in memory of me" might be rendered as "do this as my memorial". This is the great memorial, *anamnesis* in Greek, that is, a re-presentation or even a "replay" in modern English. This is not just remembering in the head, "a memory", still less a memorial plaque set on a wall or a

monument in a cemetery, rather it is a re-presentation or re-enactment that makes the great event from the past present among us now.

When they celebrate the Passover in their families, our Jewish brothers and sisters have a sense of entering into their liberation from Egypt in a great memorial. Hence we see why, faithful to that understanding, the Church teaches that each Mass literally makes our liberation through Calvary and Easter present here among us at the altar. The Mass is the great "replay" bringing the Cross into our time and space, re-presenting and applying the power of the Cross as perfect prayer for the living and the dead.

At the time of the Reformation this interpretation was replaced by a European psychological idea of "remembering", hence the translation "do this *in remembrance* of me". The Mass was replaced by a Lord's Supper, a symbolic meal of bread and wine when believers remember the saving death of Jesus. But that broke away from the ancient Jewish tradition of sacrifice, which we see embodied in the Eucharistic words of Jesus Christ and the liturgies of East and West.

However it is not true to say that the Mass is "a memorial of the Last Supper". The Mass re-enacts the Last Supper and not a literal re-enactment at that. We do not recline on divans around a horseshoe table. But as Christian worship, as liturgy, the celebration of the Eucharist derived from the Last Supper is the great memorial making Christ's sacrifice present among us now.

The witness of Saint Paul

After he passed on the words of the Lord at the Last Supper, Saint Paul affirmed: *"For as often as you eat this bread and drink the cup, you proclaim the Lord's death until he comes."* (1 Corinthians 11: 26) But the death we "proclaim" is the Sacrifice of Christ which is "shown forth" when we celebrate the Eucharist.

Saint Paul regarded the Christian Eucharist as a true sacrifice because he compared this Sacrifice to pagan sacrifices. He warned Christians at Corinth: *"...my beloved, shun the worship of idols. I speak as to sensible men; judge for you what I say. The cup of blessing which we bless, is it not a participation in the blood of Christ? The bread which we break, is it not a participation in the body of Christ? Because there is one bread, we who are many are made one body, for we all partake of the one bread."* (1 Corinthians 10:14-16). "Participation", *koinonia*, may better be translated as "communion". By offering and eating, the Eucharist, Christians enter communion with the Lord and with one another.

Then, drawing on Hebrew and pagan traditions of sacrifice, he tells the Corinthians what happens if you enter communion with false gods by sharing in their sacrifices. *"Consider the practice of Israel; are not those who eat the sacrifices partners in the altar? What do I imply then? That food offered to idols anything, or that an idol is anything? No, I imply that what pagans sacrifice they offer to demons and not to God. I do not want you to be partners with demons. You cannot drink the cup of the Lord and the cup of demons. You cannot partake of the table of the Lord and the table of demons. Shall we provoke the Lord to jealousy? Are we stronger than he?"* (1 Corinthians 10:17-22).

If Saint Paul knew that the Christian community is formed by communion in the Eucharistic Sacrifice, he was also aware of the Last Supper as a Passover meal, transformed for Christians. He says, "*…Christ, our paschal lamb, has been sacrificed. Let us therefore celebrate the festival, not with the old leaven (yeast), the leaven of malice and evil, but with the unleavened bread of sincerity and truth.*" (1 Corinthians 5:7) In the Roman Rite the Lord's Sacrifice is celebrated with unleavened bread.

The sacrifice in Tradition

We use the term "tradition" to describe the "handing on" of sacred truth and sacred action within the Church from the age of the Apostles across three millennia. St Paul spoke of this handing on of the Eucharistic tradition. Before he repeated the words of Jesus Christ at the Last Supper, he said, "*I received from the Lord what I also delivered to you…*" (1 Corinthians 11: 23). This living tradition has been handed on across the ages in the prayers and actions of the liturgies of the Catholic Church, Eastern and Western.

We do not rely on the Scriptures alone for the abiding tradition that the Eucharistic celebration is a true sacrifice.

The Second Vatican Council teaches that the Word of God comes to us through two sources, Scripture and Tradition.[16] The faith and worship of the ancient Churches of the East and the West centred around the Christian sacrifice, demonstrated by sources from the first four centuries, the texts of early liturgies and the teaching of the Fathers and Councils.

An early source is *The Didache*, a short manual of instruction for Christians, written not long after the books of the New Testament. The first generations of Christians believed that the Eucharist is a sacrifice as the text reveals. *"On the Lord's day assemble and break bread and give thanks, having first confessed your sins, that your sacrifice may be pure. If anyone has a dispute with his brother, let him not come to the assembly till they are reconciled, that your sacrifice be not polluted. For this is the sacrifice spoken of by the Lord, 'In every place and at every time offer to me a pure sacrifice; for I am a great king, said the Lord, and my name is wonderful among the nations.'* (Malachi 1:11, 14)." [17]

In his Letter to the Philadelphians, written in the same era, St Ignatius of Antioch refers to "the one altar" of the bishop. As we have seen, the Christian altar itself is a testimony to Catholic faith in the Lord's Sacrifice since earliest times. Testimony to the Eucharist as sacrifice is found in other sources: such as: St Justin Martyr, St Irenaeus, Tertullian, and St Cyprian. After the Council of

Nicaea, St Cyril of Alexandria, St Cyril of Jerusalem, St John Chrysostom, St Ambrose and St Augustine see the Eucharist as a sacrifice.

The Fathers and ancient writers present the Christian sacrifice as "spiritual", that is, different to material offerings of animals. Through unity with Christ in the Eucharist Christians offer themselves to God. Their baptismal lives have a sacrificial quality, particularly relevant in the age of the martyrs.

This sacrificial tradition was passed on in the liturgies. Writing on the sacraments in the mid Fourth Century, St Ambrose of Milan provided much of the text of the Roman Canon (First Eucharistic Prayer). The sacrificial language used at altars in Fourth Century Rome and Milan is clearer in the re-translated English text: "...*we, your servants and your holy people, offer to your glorious majesty from the gifts that you have given us, this pure victim, this holy victim, this spotless victim, the holy Bread of eternal life, and the Chalice of everlasting salvation.*"

The work of Christ, Priest and Lamb

Scripture and Traditon testify to the Eucharistic Sacrifice of Jesus Christ, who is both Priest and Lamb as we see in the Gospel of St John. In John 6:25-29 he promises his *"flesh"* and *"blood"*, sacrificial food *"which I shall give for the life of the world"*. There is a sacrificial theme in the teaching which is the Lord's own affirmation of his Real Presence. However, in St John's Gospel, in the account of the Last Supper we do not find the Eucharistic words of the Lord, rather he offers himself, and consecrates himself in the beautiful "high priestly prayer" (cf. John 17).[18] Here he anticipates his self-sacrifice on the following day, Good Friday.

Christ, the High Priest

The theme of Jesus the High Priest in central to the Letter to the Hebrews, which inspires scholars seeking to understand his Eucharistic Sacrifice. This is why the opening chapters of the letter spell out the Incarnation, that God the Son willingly took human flesh in Jesus Christ. Because he is God and Man, divine and human, he becomes the priest-mediator or bridge between God and humanity. In atonement for our sins he offers *his body*, his whole humanity, to the Father, and brings our human nature into the dimensions of heaven, which is depicted in the Letter as if it were the great Temple in Jerusalem. The self-giving of Christ in eternity reveals Christ not only as the Priest who offers and a willing Victim but as the Temple and Altar of sacrifice.[19] His body is likened to the torn veil of the Temple, for through his pierced flesh we have access to God. In the Eucharistic Sacrifice he instituted at the Last Supper he is the eternal Priest "of the order of Melchisedech".

We tend to think of bringing the sacrifice of Christ down to our altars, but the Letter to the Hebrews offers another way of understanding the Eucharistic Sacrifice. Through the earthly liturgy Christ our High Priest raises us into his eternal sacrifice in heaven, into the very heart of God the Trinity. Through the liturgy we join the compassionate High Priest who has brought his self offering of our human nature into the heart of God. He is our perfect representative before God.

The Letter to the Hebrews emphasizes the active intentional role of Christ offering himself up to the Father. To complement the Priesthood of Christ we turn to a passive image, the Lamb of God, the humble Victim.

Christ, the Lamb of God

Lambs were and are sacrificed for the Passover. At the Last Supper Jesus Christ transformed the Passover of the Old Covenant with Israel into the Eucharist of his new

Covenant with a new Israel, his Church. He became *"Christ our paschal lamb"* who *"has been sacrificed"*, as Saint Paul put it. At the table of the Last Supper and on the Cross he is the "Lamb of God". In the account of the Passion in Saint John's Gospel, the crucifixion coincides with the sacrifice of the Passover lambs. Yet these lambs were not sin-bearing sacrifices. This is where Jesus adapted the sacrificial system. He brought both Temple and Passover together in his new sacrifice of the Eucharist.

In liturgies of the East and West, Jesus Christ is described as the "Lamb of God". In the Ordinary (unchanging part) of the Roman Mass we address him as the Lamb of God in the Gloria. This is taken up again in the *Agnus Dei*: *"Lamb of God you take away the sins of the world, have mercy on us… grant us peace."* The Lord is greeted as the sacrificed Lamb while the Host is broken at the fraction in the ordinary form of Mass. The *Agnus Dei* is said just before the priest's Communion in the extraordinary form of the Mass. In both forms of the Roman rite, the priest invites the people to Holy Communion holding the Host before them and echoing the words of Saint John the Baptist: *"Behold the Lamb of God, behold him who takes away the sins of the world."* (cf. John 1:29).

The Lamb of God presents Jesus as the Paschal (Passover) Lamb, sacrificed, slain, pierced for us, with not a bone of his body broken, in accord with Passover rule and custom. As we have seen, Paul takes this up for: "*Christ our Passover is sacrificed for us…*" (1 Corinthians 5:7). The unblemished Lamb is also found in 1 Peter 1:19.

In the Book of Revelation John's metaphor of the Lamb is used repeatedly, culminating in the echo of Ephesians 5, the "Marriage of the Lamb" in the glory of heaven (cf. Revelation 19-22). But this depends on sacrificial imagery because the Lamb has first been revealed, "*as it were slain*", yet living for ever (cf Revelation 5:6; 13:8). As in the priestly imagery of the Letter to the Hebrews, Christ's victimhood, accomplished on the Cross is made present eternally before the Father. This is set out in Eucharistic Prayer III in prayer to God the Father: "*Look we pray upon the oblation of the Church and recognizing the sacrificial Victim by whose death you willed to reconcile us to yourself…*"

The Lamb of God, "Broken for You"

Various Eastern liturgies include the words "broken for you" rather than "given up for you". Both expressions convey a sacrificial meaning because "given up for you" and "broken for you" are virtually equivalent. But the emphasis on "breaking" raises another question, the meaning of the "breaking of the bread". Does this also symbolize the Lord's Sacrifice?

The "breaking of the bread" or fraction in the Roman Rite is a practical prelude to the community sharing Holy

Communion. It expresses the truth taught by Saint Paul, that many members of the community who share in the one Bread make up one body and become one body.[20] The fraction is not regarded as a symbol of the death of Christ, even if the singing or recitation of *Agnus Dei* accompanies this moment. Moreover, in the Passover tradition not a bone of the sacrificed lambs was broken.

By contrast, liturgies of the East find sacrificial symbolism in "the breaking of the bread". In the Byzantine Rite, this is carried out in two moments. Before the Divine Liturgy begins, the priest goes to the table of prothesis to the left of the altar. Saying the prayers of the Office of the Prothesis he prepares the leavened bread and the chalice of wine. He cuts out the main portion of bread, *amnos*, "the Lamb", using explicit sacrificial language: *"The Lamb of God who takes away the sins of the world is immolated for the life and salvation of the world."* He pierces the Lamb saying: *"One of the soldiers pierced his side with a lance, and at once there came forth blood and water…"* He then blesses the chalice of wine and water that has been prepared by the deacon. He goes on to divide up the loaf, arranging small portions on the paten to represent Our Lady and the saints.

During the central prayers of the Divine Liturgy the priest repeats the Last Supper narrative of consecration, prays the great memorial, *anamnesis*, and invokes the Holy Spirit to change the bread and wine into the Body and

Blood of the Lord, *epiklesis*. Then he breaks "the Lamb", saying: "*Broken and distributed is the Lamb of God, broken and not dismembered, always eaten and never expended, but making holy those who receive it.*"

In a Passover tradition the slain lamb then becomes a "mystical supper" for the faithful who receive the Lord. The immolation of the Paschal Lamb brings the sacrifice, and the sacred banquet, into harmony. The rich symbolic liturgical action of the Byzantine Rite is celebrated by millions of Christians, Catholic and Orthodox, perpetuating John's vivid metaphor of the Lamb of God and revealing that the Sacrifice is at the heart of the Divine Liturgy.

If consecrated leavened bread is described as "the Lamb" in the Byzantine Rite, in the Roman Rite consecrated unleavened bread is called the "Host", from the Latin word "*hostia*", meaning a "victim". Bringing East and West together, Catholics believe that Jesus the Lamb of God is victim and priest in his eternal Sacrifice, made present whenever the Eucharist is celebrated, no matter what rite is used.

Questions to resolve

The Lord's Sacrifice raises questions which theologians have attempted to answer. None of these answers is complete, because the Eucharist always remains "The Mystery of Faith". Yet saints and scholars have deepened our understanding of what Christ the Priest and Lamb accomplishes on our altars.

Sacrifice or meal?

Jesus commanded his own to "take and eat" the bread changed into his Body and to drink the wine changed into his Blood. This is why we hear some people say that "the Mass is a meal". This assertion can be traced back to the mid-twentieth century liturgical movement in France. So is the Eucharist a community meal, rather than a sacrifice? This may explain why some people say "Eucharist" (without a definite article) instead of "Mass", even when this does not quite make sense. However, it is not true to our tradition and very misleading to make a meal the model for the Eucharistic Liturgy. It even risks reducing the sacramental mystery to something ordinary. A "meal" in our culture can mean anything from a feast to a snack.

The Mass is both a sacrifice and a meal, as we saw the symbolism of the altar. The altar reminds us that is not a matter of "either" "or". The Mass is both the saving sacrifice and a sacred meal. The signs, actions and language of liturgy reveal the Eucharist as the Lord's Sacrifice and the Lord's Banquet, a sacred offering and a sacred meal in one action of worship. But the Mass is *primarily* the Sacrifice of the Lord, evident in his own Eucharistic words.

At the Second Vatican Council, the priority of the sacrifice was set out in the *Constitution on the Sacred Liturgy*: "*At the last Supper, on the night he was betrayed, our Saviour instituted the Eucharistic sacrifice of his Body and Blood. This he did in order to perpetuate the Sacrifice of the Cross throughout the ages until he should cone again and so to entrust to his beloved Spouse, the Church, a memorial of his death and Resurrection: a sacrament, of love, a sign of unity, a Paschal banquet 'in which Christ is consumed, the mind is filled with grace, and a pledge of future glory is given to us'.*"[21]

It might be said that the Mass is the Sacrifice of the Lord in the form of a holy meal, or, better still, that the Liturgy of Sacrifice is completed by the "spiritual banquet" of receiving the Eucharist. A "banquet" is closer to the festive meaning of sharing the Eucharist. In his *O sacrum convivium* St Thomas Aquinas praises the Eucharistic mystery: "*O sacred banquet, in which Christ is received, the memory of his passion is renewed, the mind is filled with grace and a pledge of future glory is given to us.*"

"Banquet" also captures something of a marriage feast, drawing us to look forward to the "Supper of the Lamb" in heaven. This brings together the sacrificed Lamb and receiving sacred food. As the priest shows the people the broken Host he says *"Behold the Lamb of God, behold him who takes away the sins of the world. Blessed are those called to the supper of the Lamb."* The word "supper" also has different meanings, again showing how difficult it is to find an English word for this sacred eating and drinking. In the vision of heaven in the Book of Revelation the "Supper of the Lamb" is a marriage feast or nuptial banquet. In Van Eyck's great altarpiece "The Supper of the Lamb", the slain Lamb of God is depicted standing on a beautifully vested late medieval altar. The Lamb points us back to the Passover sacrifices that are fulfilled in the Eucharistic Sacrifice.

The Fathers of the Synod on the Eucharist, 2005, were conscious of this question of sacrifice and meal. In a brief intervention in the earliest phase of the Synod, Pope Benedict XVI responded to questions raised by some bishops about the sacrifice and meal. The Pope took the Synod back to the Passover, a ritual, a sacred meal, not a secular meal. He underlined the fact this sacred meal depends on and is inseparable from the sacrifice of the lambs that are eaten at the Passover table.

The communion sacrifice

At the same time, in the Jerusalem Temple there was a form of sacrifice that was completed by a shared meal and this has great significance for our understanding of the Eucharistic Sacrifice. In *communion sacrifices* parts of the victim were cooked and shared as holy food by the priest and by those offering the gift through the priest at the altar. Such a sacred banquet joined them to the Holy God of Israel and to one another in a covenant unity, in a sacred communion. There was a practical purpose for this kind of sacrifice. It is a religious way of sealing an agreement between two parties. By this sacred eating those making the offering were joined to God and bound to one another. As Saint Paul reminded the Corinthians: *"Consider the practice of Israel; are not those who eat the sacrifices partners in the altar"* (1 Corinthians 10:18).

The Last Supper reflects the "communion sacrifice" when Our Lord commands his Church to offer up and then eat and drink his Body and Blood. Through this sacred eating and drinking we are most perfectly and completely united to the Sacrifice of Christ. We offer ourselves in communion with him to the loving Father, who we addressed as "our Father" at the beginning of the Communion Rite. Thus it is through receiving the sacrament of the Eucharist, or Holy Communion, that we share most fully in the Sacrifice of the Lord.

One sacrifice or many?

The Church teaches that the Mass is the same Sacrifice as the Cross. At the Council of Trent, the bishops taught that: *"One and the same is the victim, now offered through the ministry of priests, who offered himself on the cross, only the way the offering is made is different"*. This means that in each Mass, the one all-sufficient Sacrifice of Jesus Christ is offered, but in an "un-bloody" or sacramental form.

In the historical event of his freely chosen death, Jesus Christ gained our salvation once and for all. But *the way* we receive the benefits of this death is the Eucharistic Sacrifice. This is the channel of the Grace of salvation. This is the way Christ chose to perpetuate and apply to us his saving work, here and now in the time and place where we live. Citing a liturgical prayer, the Second Vatican Council taught: *"As often as the Sacrifice of the Cross by which 'Christ our Pasch is sacrificed' (1 Corinthians 5:7) is celebrated on the altar, the work of our redemption is carried out."*[22]

Aware of Catholic teaching in a superficial way, anti-Catholic Fundamentalists allege that Catholics believe that Jesus "dies again" in each Mass. They say that we believe he is re-crucified by the priest on the altar, hence they assert that our Mass is a blasphemous repetition of the once-and-for-all sacrifice of Jesus on the Cross. They say that we presume to add something to the finished work of Christ on Calvary.

We agree that there is only One Sacrifice, the self-immolation of Jesus Christ on the Cross. But, as Christians have always believed since New Testament times, we hold that every celebration of the Eucharist is the re-presentation or Memorial of his one Sacrifice. Jesus said "*do this in memory of me*", or more precisely, "do this as my memorial". As I have indicated, the Greek word "memorial", *anamnesis*, should be understood not in the sense of remembering something but as the Jews understand it, in the vivid biblical sense of a real "re-play" of the saving acts of God. This great memorial makes Christ's work for us present again. Each Mass is not a mere "remembrance" of the death of Christ but a supernatural re-enactment and re-presentation of his completed saving work on the cross.[23]

We may therefore say that at every Mass we are once more on the hill of Calvary. We stand with Mary and John, with the courageous women, with Mary Magdalene and the centurion, with the faithful ones, the doubting ones, even the confused ones who wondered what was happening. At every Mass, we also gather with them at the empty tomb when the suffering and doubting ceased, because his Sacrifice was his victory over sin and death. The whole of Christ's work for us, the "Paschal Mystery", is contained in the Mass – his life, death and resurrection, yet the central pivot of the Paschal Mystery is always the self-giving death of the Lord on the Cross.

Just after the consecration in every Eucharistic Prayer, the great memorial is recalled. In the First Eucharistic Prayer or Roman Canon: *"we celebrate the memorial of the blessed Passion, the Resurrection from the dead, and the glorious Ascension into heaven of Christ, your Son, our Lord…"* In the Third Eucharistic Prayer a future dimension is added as *"we look forward to his second coming"*. Likewise in the first acclamation: *"We proclaim your death, O Lord, and profess your Resurrection until you come again."*

The future is also included in the Liturgy of Saint John Chrysostom *"Remembering therefore this saving command and all that was done for our sake, the cross, the tomb, the resurrection on the third day, the ascension into heaven, the enthronement at the right hand, the second and glorious coming again, we offer you your own, from what is yours, in all and for the sake of all."*

Memorial encompasses past events, God's saving acts in history, and points us to the future. When we examine theologies that attempt to explain how the Mass is a sacrifice, we will also encounter another dimension of Memorial, the question of the relationship between time and eternity, earth and heaven.

What is the purpose of this Holy Sacrifice?

In the First Eucharistic Prayer the Mass is described as *"this sacrifice of praise"*. The word "Eucharist" means "thanksgiving". Christians offer praise and thanks to God the Father in the Liturgy. The Eucharistic Prayer, Canon or Anaphora is the "Great Thanksgiving", hence introduced with "*Let us give thanks to the Lord our God*" to which we respond "*It is right and just.*" In the preface that follows, the priest gives thanks for the saving work of God in Christ, with words appropriate to the feast day, season or specific occasion.

However, at the time of the Reformation, Martin Luther said that the Mass is only a sacrifice of praise and thanksgiving. In the teaching and practice of the Church it is much more as we saw in the Eucharistic words of Jesus at the Last Supper. The Eucharistic liturgy is the all-powerful pleading of the Passion of Christ on the Cross; therefore the Church describes the Mass as the Sacrifice of *propitiation*, that is, the gaining of the Father's loving favour and mercy for sinners. The Third Eucharistic Prayer speaks of "*this sacrifice of our reconciliation.*" Through the Mass, we apply the reconciling and saving death and resurrection of our Lord to help the living and the dead, to gain mercy, pardon and peace.

The sacrifice of Christ Priest and Lamb is offered for specific "ends" or purposes. These are all derived from the redeeming work of Christ on the Cross and the intentions of his eternal Priesthood expressed in his words at the Last Supper. The Mass is offered for four ends:

1. *to adore God and give him glory*, so the Eucharistic sacrifice is the act of perfect worship and praise;

2. *in thanksgiving for all God's gifts*, hence the term 'Eucharist', so it is the act of perfect gratitude, of grateful praise;

3. *to make intercession for all our needs*, so it is the act of perfect prayer, the Great Prayer of Christ in us, his Church praying for the world;

4. *to make atonement for the sins of the living and the dead*, so the Mass is a sacrifice of propitiation, gaining pardon, peace and reconciliation for the living and the dead.

The power of the Mass is infinite because his atoning Sacrifice on the cross has infinite value. Whether celebrated in solemn splendor in a glorious cathedral or in the simplicity of a humble chapel, the Mass has the same infinite value. Before this mystery, and approaching it in faith, we should wonder and marvel at the generosity of the Divine Mercy shown forth every day on the altars of the Church.

Catholics have Masses celebrated for special intentions, above all for the dead. Each separate celebration of the Holy Sacrifice, as it were, applies, directs and focuses the saving power of Christ's cross and resurrection to a specific purpose. Through the perfect prayer of the Mass we can reach out in merciful love to our dear departed, bridging the gulf of death that separates them from us. We can "do something" for them, helping them as they are being purified and prepared for heaven. Yet all the while we are only cooperating in and benefiting from one great Gift of mercy that God has granted us in his Son, the work of the Lord Jesus, Redeemer of the world and only Saviour of humanity.

But how is the Mass a sacrifice?

If the Mass is the same Sacrifice as the Cross, the Church has largely left the explanation of *how* this is so to sacramental theologians and liturgists. Various theories as to how the Mass is the Sacrifice of Christ usually focus on some "moment" during the liturgy when we can say that the Lord's Sacrifice is being offered.

However first of all a common misunderstanding must be eliminated. The Eucharistic sacrifice is not offering God some bread and wine. That would make the Mass no better than the cereal offerings in the Temple. Those sacrifices of grain and fruit were brought to an end at the Last Supper. At the "offertory" or Preparation of the Offerings the priest offers bread and wine, but only as the raw materials, as it were, for the real sacrifice. There is a marvelous exchange when the bread and wine we have presented to the Father is returned to us as the true Body and Blood of his Son, but that exchange is not the sacrifice even if it is a way of understanding how the Liturgy of the Eucharist unfolds.

The exchange of gifts begins in the offertory, when Christ took the bread and wine into his hands. Now these gifts are offerings. In the Eucharistic Prayer, or canon, we repeat his next action, blessing or giving thanks, and the offerings are changed into his Body and Blood. In the third stage, sharing Holy Communion, we obey his command to eat and drink. These acts are stages in an unfolding sacrificial action. But this still leaves open the question: at what point does this act of worship become the Lord's Sacrifice?

Theologies of sacrifice

The first attempt to define the moment of sacrifice could be described as "the medieval destruction theory". Theologians tried to find an essential part of the Mass that represented the *death* of a sacrificial victim. Unfortunately this school of thought failed to understand the Hebrew concept of sacrifice. The act of killing a victim, or its death, was not the sacrifice. It was offering God the life force or the blood that had been released or "poured out" by slaying that constituted a sacrifice.

Theologians who regarded death or destruction as the sacrifice proposed various moments in the Mass as the offering of the sacrifice. Some suggested the "destruction" of the substance of bread and wine through transubstantiation at the consecration, others the mingling of a fragment of the Host in the Blood of Christ, or even the breaking of the Host. Some argued that eating and drinking Christ's Body and Blood was the sacrifice. However, none of these moments could be the essential sacrifice because most of them only affect the outward appearances (species) of bread and wine. A less literal idea of destruction saw the separation of the Body and Blood of Christ as a mystical immolation.

In the Seventeenth and Eighteenth centuries the Mass was seen as the celestial immolation of Christ made present on earth. The model for this was the "heavenly session", that is, Christ the Priest and Lamb adoring his Father, but some theologians said that the priestly symbolism of Christ in heaven should not be taken literally.

The oblation or "offering" theologies of the Eucharistic sacrifice marked a more sophisticated development. Influenced by the liturgical movement of the Twentieth Century, theologians led by M. de la Taille[24] rightly argued that destroying a victim does not constitute the essence of a sacrifice, rather some *intentional act* of offering. They could cite the Letter to the Hebrews which, as we have seen, described an eternal heavenly oblation made consciously and willingly by Christ the High Priest. They said that this self-offering in God is made present on earth in each Mass. They could cite the Roman Canon, Eucharistic Prayer I, when the celebrant prays that the gifts be "*borne by the hands of your holy Angel to your altar on high*". The "Angel" is an ancient symbolic reference to Christ the Priest.

There is a great truth here. While completed in time once and for all on the Cross, the self-offering of Christ on the Cross is itself an eternal "action" within God the Holy Trinity. In the Trinity, the Son offers himself to the Father through the Holy Spirit. This great outpouring of eternal love is, as it were "at the heart of" God. In the Roman liturgy the eternal love between Three Divine Persons who are One is summed up and proclaimed in the great doxology (act of praise) at the end of the Eucharistic Prayer: "*Through him and with him and in him, O God, almighty Father, in the unity of the Holy Spirit, all glory and honor is yours, for ever and ever…*"

As the priest sings or says these words, Christ's eternal self-offering is symbolically represented. He raises the Chalice and Host together, not to show them to people, as happens at the elevations after the consecration, rather to symbolize the offering of the one perfect Sacrifice.

Theologians of great stature favored the oblation school of thought which draws on the riches of the liturgy. However, it ran into historical and logical difficulties once it required that the priest must recite some specific liturgical formula such as "*we offer you, Lord, the Bread of life and the Chalice of salvation*" and not just the Lord's words at the consecration, so as to achieve a "true moment" of sacrifice during the Mass. This partly explains why the prevailing theology of sacrifice today follows a simpler course by focusing more on the words of consecration, that is, what happens through the wondrous change of bread and wine that we call transubstantiation.

Pope Paul VI focused on the consecration of the bread and wine as the offering of the Eucharistic Sacrifice. *"The Lord's immolation in the sacrifice of the Mass without bloodshed, his symbolic presentation of the sacrifice of the cross and his application of its saving virtue, all these take place at the moment when, by the words of consecration, he begins to be present sacramentally, as the spiritual food of the faithful under the appearances of bread and wine."*[25] This may be summed up: the Sacrifice of the Lord is made present through the consecration of bread and wine, his Body and his Blood, offered for us.

The double consecration of bread and wine constitutes the offering of the sacrifice because this makes Christ Priest and Lamb really present among us. We cannot separate the Real Presence from the Real Sacrifice. His eternal self-offering is made present among us in every Mass. As we have seen, the Jewish mind would understand that the separate consecration of bread and wine also represents his state of being a victim just as it represents his intentional action as the true Priest of a New Covenant, which the oblation school of thought rightly emphasized.

Time and eternity

However, we find a different approach among Eastern Christians. Here there is little trace of the Western quest for a "moment" of sacrifice. The whole celebration of the Divine Liturgy is the worship of heaven made present on earth, into which we humbly enter, admitted through Baptism. This is why the Lamb of God theme begins in the preparation of the bread and wine before the priest proceeds into the liturgy of word and sacrifice and before the faithful are called to "mystical supper" of the Lamb.

Eastern Christian worship opens another door into the Eucharistic Sacrifice. It helps us reflect on the relationship between time and eternity, between what we do on this earth and the eternal self-giving in God the Trinity in heaven. What happened once and for all in time, on Calvary, is always "there" in the timelessness of God. We are taken into the eternal worship of heaven through the visible signs and symbols of liturgy.

This applies equally to the sacrifice and the banquet. Jesus Christ, God and Man, under the appearances of bread and wine, is both offering his eternal Sacrifice and providing himself as food for our pilgrimage in time and our passing into eternal life after death. Here at the altar the world of matter and time intersects with eternal worship, or we might say that earth and heaven overlap in every Mass.

A wondrous mystery

Surely we must wonder and marvel when time and eternity overlap. But the wonder rises from what is really happening at the altar. Once we understand what is happening, we realize that, through the Liturgy, we encounter the divine here and now in our world. This calls for reflection, meditation and understanding, but always with a sense of awe. The Eucharist as sacrifice and sacrament can never be completely understood. The Eucharist always remains the "tremendous and fascinating Mystery" – the divine work we proclaim as *the Mystery of Faith*.

Liturgy, sacrifice and beauty

The Sacrifice of Christ, Priest and Lamb is always beautiful in itself, for *God is beautiful*. God's goodness is expressed in the beauty of creation and the work of redemption which finds a "summit and source" in the holy Eucharist. But some argue that artistic and decorative elements in liturgy, such as fine vestments and vessels, are additions to worship which detract from its essence. This is a misguided and ultimately destructive opinion.

Liturgy is not merely an outer wrapping or a decorative package around the essence of the Mass, so-called "externals" of worship. Catholics of the Eastern Rites teach us much here. They call the celebration of the Eucharist the "Divine Liturgy", that is, the sacred duty God has given us, and they see this action as God's great act of worship running through the whole of creation and on into eternity. In the Eastern traditions, God invites us into his worship. It is not just what we do. In the liturgy, we enter heaven when we obey the Lord and re-enact the Last Supper with the solemn and majestic ceremonies of the Church.

For Eastern Christians ceremonies are not "externals" but the normal way of offering the Holy Sacrifice. The ceremonies include reverent gestures, fine music, using sacred vessels, lights, incense, noble vestments, and all this detail is found in a noble setting, a church filled with icons, frescoes or mosaics. A tradition of symbolism is integral to Christian sacramental worship, because signs and symbols take us up into heavenly worship. We join Our Lady, the saints and angels and all the company of heaven around us in the icons. The language of our Roman Rite says that, but in practice the way our Western form of the Mass is celebrated today can become dull and colorless. The sacred, the sense of the divine mysteries, may even be obscured by a cool rational approach that focuses on essentials.

It has been said that "It is the Mass that matters" and to make it matter we focus on the sacrificial mystery in itself. But we should respect the beauty that arouses a sense of "wonder and awe" before the miracle of God among us,

God working through us, in us, God transforming us. This has more to do with silence, prayer and a sense of reverence, but it calls for offering God the best of human culture in art and music.

The beauty of the Eucharistic celebration flows from the simple action entrusted to us at the Last Supper, the offering of Christ's saving Sacrifice. This has been developed and enriched by many Christian cultures across the centuries in our liturgical traditions, Western or Eastern. The beauty of the Mass is expressed in reverent ceremonial and good music, even if it is never entirely dependent on them.

Therefore the Mass can present simple or complex forms of beauty, depending on the circumstances and occasion. Catholics can discover a great spiritual beauty in a simple group Mass at a youth camp in a forest or in a solemn high Mass sung by a choir in a soaring Gothic cathedral. The Mass can be related to this world and at the same time seem "other-worldly" – which is what the seven sacraments are all about. Christ the Priest and Lamb is always the bridge between heaven and earth.

The Mass seems natural when looked at from one angle, supernatural from another, like a perfectly cut jewel that varies with the refracted light and continually reveals its hidden glories in new situations or when it is seen from different aspects. Let us therefore never take the Lord's Sacrifice for granted, or make it a matter of habit or routine.

Let us allow this divine treasure to surprise us and then we may understand what Blessed John Henry Newman meant when he described the Mass as "the most beautiful thing this side of heaven".

In humble reverence

Great truths and beautiful sacred realities call for respectful language. We should refer to *the* Eucharist and not just say "Eucharist". The Eucharist is the greatest of all seven Sacraments. Putting "Holy" or "Blessed" in front of "Eucharist" helps underline that this is the source and summit of Christian life. Holy Communion" is still an official liturgical description of the Sacrament, for example, lay men and women designated by the bishop to assist in distributing the Eucharist are "Extraordinary Ministers of Holy Communion".

It is also respectful to refer to the celebration of the Eucharist as "the Holy Sacrifice of the Mass". Language helps cultivate a sense of wonder which should flow into our lives from the Eucharistic mysteries. This wonder may also include a sense of our own unique value as created human persons because this sublime mystery passes through human hands. This is also a serious responsibility.

It is not for us to manipulate God's gift, hence the grave abuse involved in playing around with the liturgy by deliberately changing what the Church has passed on to us.

We are not meant to control the liturgy, treating it as if it were our creation.

However, if the Church passes the Mass on to each generation, ultimately the Holy Sacrifice comes from God the Trinity. The Mass is the worship of the Trinity into which you and I are raised when God gathers us at the altar. Strictly speaking, we do not make the Eucharist happen – we share in what is happening, God working through priest and people.

We are to be humble before the Mystery of Faith, this gift of God. Yet, at the same time, we should recognize our self-worth through the offering of the Eucharistic Sacrifice. We come from fallen stock; we need to be redeemed, but our dignity as Christian men and women far outweighs that fall. God's grace is perfecting our nature. That is a Eucharistic understanding of the human person.

Therefore the essential optimism of the Catholic understanding of the human person shines through the Holy Sacrifice of the Mass. Jesus Christ, Priest and Lamb, is saying that this Sacrifice is offered "*for you*" and his command to "*do this*" empowers his Church, but he also expresses great trust and confidence in our capacity "*do this*" well. This trust should encourage each of us to ask how we can value the Mass more and how the sacrificial mysteries of the altar can add meaning and value to our daily lives as Christians.

End notes

[1] Linking an altar to the tomb of a saint went back to when Mass was celebrated over the tombs of martyrs, perhaps in the Catacombs. We still maintain this link by inserting the relics of saints in or under a new altar during the rite of dedication.

[2] Cf. Joseph Ratzinger, *The Feast of Faith*, Ignatius Press, San Francisco, 1980, p. 145 and *The Spirit of the Liturgy*, Ignatius Press, San Francisco, 2000, pp. 83-84.

[3] *General Instruction of the Roman Missal*, revised text, nos. 117, 122, 308.

[4] Which is why altars were demolished at the English Reformation. See Eamon Duffy, *The Stripping of the Altars*, Yale University press 1992, pp. 472, 555-557, 568, 583.

[5] As argued by Dom Gregory Dix in *The Shape of the Liturgy*, Dacre Press, London, 1945-1960. pp 16-27.

[6] See *Benedict XVI* and *Beauty in Sacred Art and Architecture*, Four Courts Press, Dublin, 2011, Helen Ratner Dietz, "The Nuptial meaning of Classical Church Architecture", pp 122-126.

[7] Second Vatican Council, *Sacrosanctum Concilium*, 7.

[8] See *General Instruction of the Roman Missal*, revised text n. 295. There never has been any official directive to remove altar rails.

[9] Second Vatican Council, *Decree on the Ministry and Life of Priests*, 2.

[10] See, Joseph Ratzinger, *The Spirit of the Liturgy*, Ignatius Press, Part 1. chapter 1, "Liturgy and Life", pp. 15-19.

[11] This was vividly seen in the Eucharistic way the Personal Ordinariate for former Anglicans was inaugurated in 2011

[12] This particular Passover meal was eaten before the exact day of the Passover. There has been much scholarly debate and discussion about this mystery, with various plausible explanations.

[13] The Douai Rheims translation of *tradetur* of 1 Corinthians 11: 23 uses "deliver".

[14] This is equivalent to the Latin *tradere* in the Eucharistic Prayers which is why the Latin Vulgate Bible renders the Galatians text as "he gave himself up", *tradidit se ipsum*.

[15] The Exodus verses are read on the Solemnity of Corpus Christi in the second year of the cycle of readings when the sacrificial dimension of the Eucharist is emphasized.

[16] Cf. Second Vatican Council, Dogmatic Constitution on Divine Revelation, *Dei Verbum*, 9, 10.

[17] *The Didache*, 14, Second Century A.D.

[18] For a new explanation why there is no record of the words of institution in the Gospel of John see Anthony A. La Femina, *Eucharist and Covenant in John's Last Supper Account,* New Hope Publications, US, 2011.

[19] See Albert Vanhoye, *Christ Our High Priest,* Gracewing 2011. Cardinal Vanhoye, former Rector of the Pontifical Biblical Institute, gave these Lenten reflections to the Roman Curia in 2008.

[20] As explained in the *General Instruction of the Roman Missal*, revised text 83, old text 56c.

[21] Second Vatican Council, *Sacrosanctum Concilium*, 47.

[22] Second Vatican Council, *Lumen Gentium* 3 and *Sacrosanctum Concilium 2*, citing the Secret Prayer for Mass on the Ninth Sunday after Pentecost, the Prayer Over the Offerings for the Second Sunday in Ordinary Time in the Missal of Paul VI.

[23] The *Catechism of the Catholic Church*, nos. 1362-1372, brings out this concept of "memorial".

[24] See, M. de la Taille, *Mysterium Fidei*, Paris 1931.

[25] Pope Paul VI, Encyclical Letter *Mysterium Fidei*, 34.